ENGLISH/RUSSIAN

The TODDLER'S handbOOk

with over 100 Words that every kid should know

by Dayna Martin

АНГЛИЙСКИЙ / РУССКИЙ

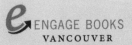
ENGAGE BOOKS
VANCOUVER

THIRD EDITION / FIRST PRINTING

Mailing address
PO BOX 4608
Main Station Terminal
349 West Georgia Street
Vancouver, BC
Canada, V6B 4A1

www.engagebooks.com

Written & compiled by: Dayna Martin
Edited & translated by: A.R. Roumanis
Proofread by: Oleksandr Senyk Александр Сеник, and Nataliya Yak-ovenko Наталия Яковенко
Designed by: A.R. Roumanis
Photos supplied by: Shutterstock
Photo on page 47 by: Faye Cornish

LIBRARY AND ARCHIVES CANADA CATALOGUING IN PUBLICATION

Martin, Dayna, 1983–, author
    The toddler's handbook : numbers, colors, shapes, sizes, ABC animals, opposites, and sounds, with over 100 words that every kid should know / written by Dayna Martin ; edited by A.R. Roumanis.

Issued in print and electronic formats.
Text in English and Russian.
ISBN 978-1-77226-453-1 (bound). –
ISBN 978-1-77226-454-8 (paperback). –
ISBN 978-1-77226-455-5 (pdf). –
ISBN 978-1-77226-456-2 (epub). –
ISBN 978-1-77226-457-9 (kindle)

1. Russian language – Vocabulary – Juvenile literature.
2. Vocabulary – Juvenile literature.
3. Word recognition – Juvenile literature.
I. Martin, Dayna, 1983– . Toddler's handbook.
II. Martin, Dayna, 1983– . Toddler's handbook. Russian.
III. Title.

PG2445.M367 2017   J491.781   C2017-905764-2
                                            C2017-905765-0

ABCs

4
Алфавит
Alfavit

NUMBERS

11
Числа
Chisla

COLORS

14
Цвета
Tsveta

OPPOSITES

16
Противоположности
Prativapalozhnasti

SHAPES

22
Формы
Formy

SOUNDS

24
Звуки
Zvuki

ACTIONS

28
Действия
Deystviya

EMOTIONS

30
Эмоции
Emotsii

SPORTS

32
Спортивный
Spartivnyy

ENGINES

34
Двигатели
Dvigateli

SIZES

36
Размеры
Razmery

BODY
38

Тело
Tela

TABLEWARE

40
Посуда
Pasuda

CLOTHES

42
Одежда
Adezhda

BATH TIME

44
Время купания
Vremya kupaniya

BED TIME
45
Время сна
Vremya sna
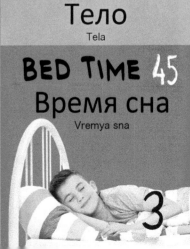
3

Aa

Alligator

Аллигатор

Alligator

Bb

Bear

Медведь

Midvet'

Cc

Cat

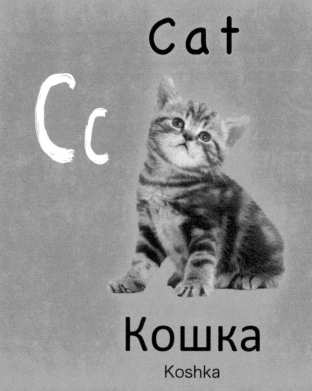

Кошка

Koshka

4

Dog
Dd

Собака
Sabaka

Fox
Ff

Лиса
Lisa

Elephant
Ee

Слон
Slon

Goat
Gg

Козёл
Kaz'ol

5

Horse

Hh

Лошадь

Loshat'

Iguana

Ii

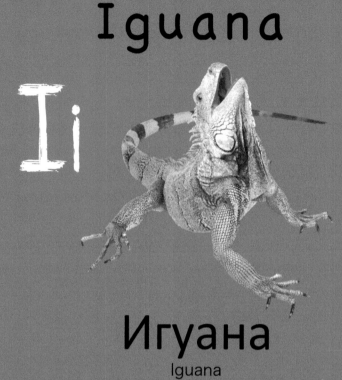

Игуана

Iguana

Jaguar

Jj

Ягуар

Yaguar

6

Koala

Kk

Коала

Koala

Lion

Ll

Лев

Lef

Mouse

Mm

Мышь

Mysh

Newt

Nn

Тритон

Triton

7

Otter

O o

Выдра
Vydra

Pig

P p

Свинья
Svin'ya

Quail

Q q

Перепел
Peripel

8

Rabbit

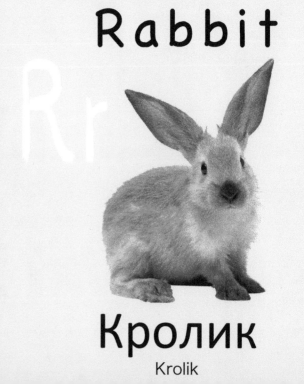

R r

Кролик
Krolik

Seal

Ss

Тюлень

Tyulen

Tiger

Tt

Тигр

Tigr

Uakari

Uu

Уакари

Uakari

Vulture

Vv

Стервятник 9

Stirvyatnik

Weasel

Ww

Ласка

Laska

X-ray fish

Xx

Рентгеновская рыба

Ringenafskaya ryba

Yak

Yy

Як

Yak

Zebra

Zz

Зебра

Zebra

Apple

One

1

Один

Odin

Яблоко

Yablaka

Crackers

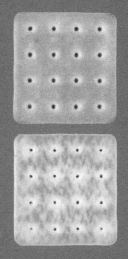

Two

2

Два

Dva

Крекеры

Krekery

Watermelon slices

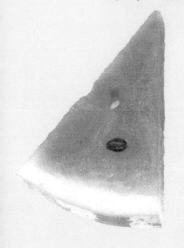  

Three

3

Три

Tri

Ломтики арбуза

Lomtiki arbuza

11

Strawberries

Four
4
Четыре
Chetyre

Клубника
Klubnika

Carrots

Five
5
Пять
Pyat

Морковь
Markof'

Tomatoes

Six
6
Шесть
Shest

Помидоры
Pamidory

Pumpkins

Seven

7

Семь

Sem

Тыквы

Tykvy

Fruit slices

Eight

8

Восемь

Vosem

Фруктовые ломтики

Fruktovyye lomtiki

Potatoes

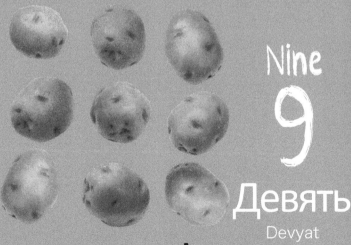

Nine

9

Девять

Devyat

Картофель

Kartofel

Cookies

Ten

10

Десять

Desyat

Печенье

Pichen' ye

13

Rainbow

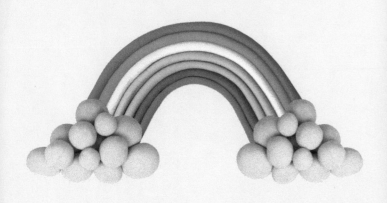

Радуга

Raduga

Red

Красный

Krasnyy

Orange

Оранжевый

Aranzhevyy

14

Yellow

Жёлтый

Zholtyy

Green

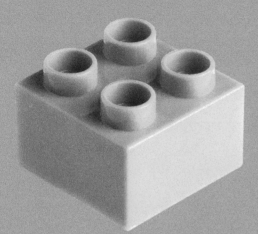

Зелёный

Zel'onyy

Blue

Синий

Siniy

Indigo

Индиго

Indigo

Violet

Фиолетовый

Fialetavyy

15

Up

Вверх
Vverkh

Down

Вниз
Vnis

In

В
V

Out

Из
Is

16

Hot

Горячий
Garyachiy

Cold

Холодный
Khalodnyy

Wet

Мокрый
Mokryy

Dry

Сухой
Sukhoy

17

Front

Передний

Piredniy

Back

Задний

Zadniy

On

18 # Включенный

Vklyuchennyy

Off

Выключенный

Vyklyuchennyy

Open

Открытый
Atkrytyy

Closed

Закрытый
Zakrytyy

Empty

Пустой
Pustoy

Full

Полный
Polnyy

19

Safe

Безопасный

Bizapasnyy

Dangerous

Опасный

Opasnyy

Big

Большой

Bal'shoy

Small

Маленький

Malen'kiy

Asleep

Спящий

Spyashchiy

Awake

Бодрствующий

Bodrstvuyushchiy

Long

Длинный

Dlinnyy

Short

Короткий

Karotkiy

21

Circle

Круг
Krug

Square

Квадрат
Kvadrat

Triangle

Треугольник
Triugol'nik

Rectangle

Прямоугольник
Pryamaugol'nik

22

Diamond

Ромб

Romp

Star

Звезда

Zvizda

Oval

Овальный

Aval'nyy

Heart

Сердце

Sertse

23

Sneeze

Ah-choo

Апчхи
Apchi

Чихать
Chikhat'

Duck

Quack

Кря
Krya

Утка
Utka

Cow

Moo

Муу
Muu

Корова
Karova

Phone

Ring

Дзынь
Dzyn'

Телефон
Tilifon

24

Monkey

Ooh-
ooh-
ahh-
ahh

Уу-уу
Uu-uu

аа-аа
aa-aa

Обезьяна
Abiz'yana

Frog

Ribbit

Ква-Ква
Kva-kva

Лягушка
Lyagushka

Hush

Shh

Тихо
Tcc- Tss

Тишина
Tishina

25

Rooster

Cock-a-doodle-doo

Ку-ка-ре-ку

Ku-ka-re-k

Петух
Pitukh

Drums

Boom

Бам-бам

Bam-bam

Барабаны
Barabany

Snake

Hiss

Ш-ш-ш

Shhhh

Змея
Zmiya

26

Owl

Hoot

Гу-гу
Gu-gu

Сова
Sava

Bumblebee

Buzz

Бзз-Bzz
Bzzzz

Шмель
Smel'

Hands

Clap

Хлоп-хлоп
Hlop-hlop

Руки
Ruki

Lamb

Baa

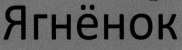

Бе-бе-бе
Be-be-be

Ягнёнок
Yegn'onok

27

Crawl

Ползать

Polzat'

Roll

Катиться

Katitsa

Walk

Ходить

Khadit'

Run

Бежать

Bizhat'

28

Hop

Прыжок
Pryzhok

Ride

Поездка
Payestka

Kiss

Поцелуй
Patseluy

Jump

Прыгать
Prygat'

29

Happy

Счастливый
Shcaslivyy

Sad

Печальный
Pichal'nyy

Angry

Сердитый
Sirdityy

Scared

Испуганный
Ispugannyy

Frustration

Разочарование

Razacharavan'ye

Surprise

Сюрприз

Syurpris

Shock

Шок

Shok

Brave

Храбрый

Khrabryy

31

Baseball

Бейсбол
Beysbol

Basketball

Баскетбол
Baskidbol

Tennis

Теннис
Tennis

Soccer

Футбол
Fudbol

Badminton

Бадминтон

Badminton

Football

Американский футбол

Amerikanskiy fudbol

Volleyball

Волейбол

Valibol

Golf

Гольф

Gol'f

33

Fire truck

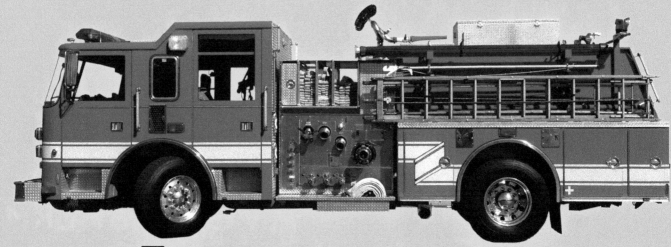

Пожарная машина

Pazharnaya mashina

Car

Автомобиль

Aftamabil'

Truck

Грузовая машина

Gruzavaya mashina

34

Helicopter

Вертолёт

Virtal'ot

Airplane

Самолёт

Samal'ot

Train

Поезд

Poist

Boat

Лодка

Lotka

35

Small   Medium   Large

Маленький Средний Большой

Malen'kiy   Sredniy   Bal'shoy

Small   Medium   Large

 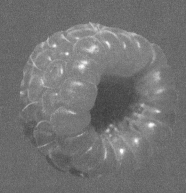 

Маленький Средний Большой

Malen'kiy   Sredniy   Bal'shoy

Large   Medium   Small

Большой   Средний   Маленький

Bal'shoy   Sredniy   Malen'kiy

Large   Medium   Small

Большой   Средний Маленький 37

Bal'shoy   Sredniy   Malen'kiy

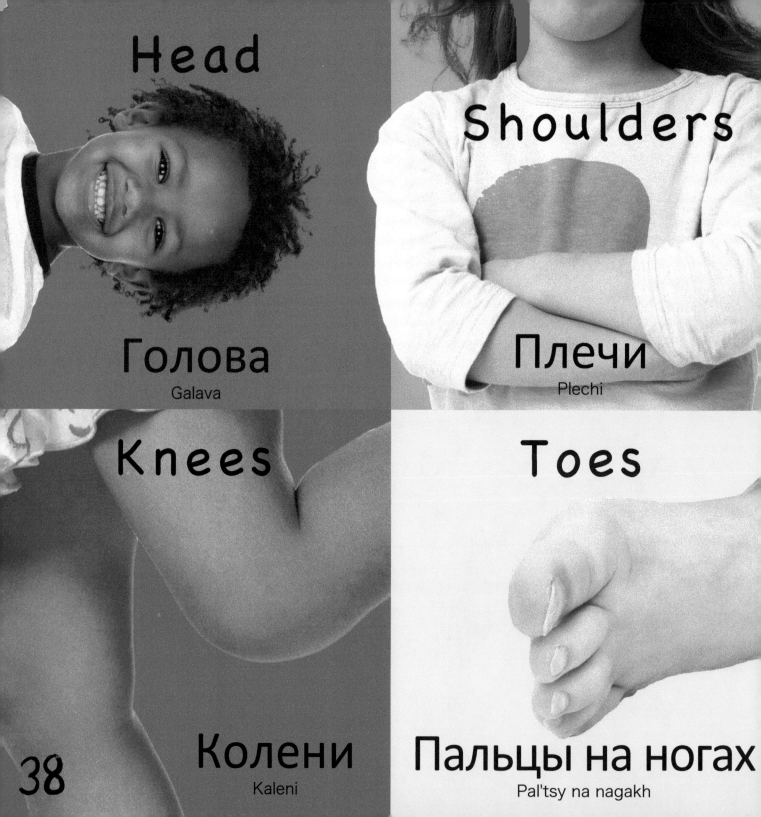

Head

Голова

Galava

Shoulders

Плечи

Plechi

Knees

Колени

Kaleni

Toes

Пальцы на ногах

Pal'tsy na nagakh

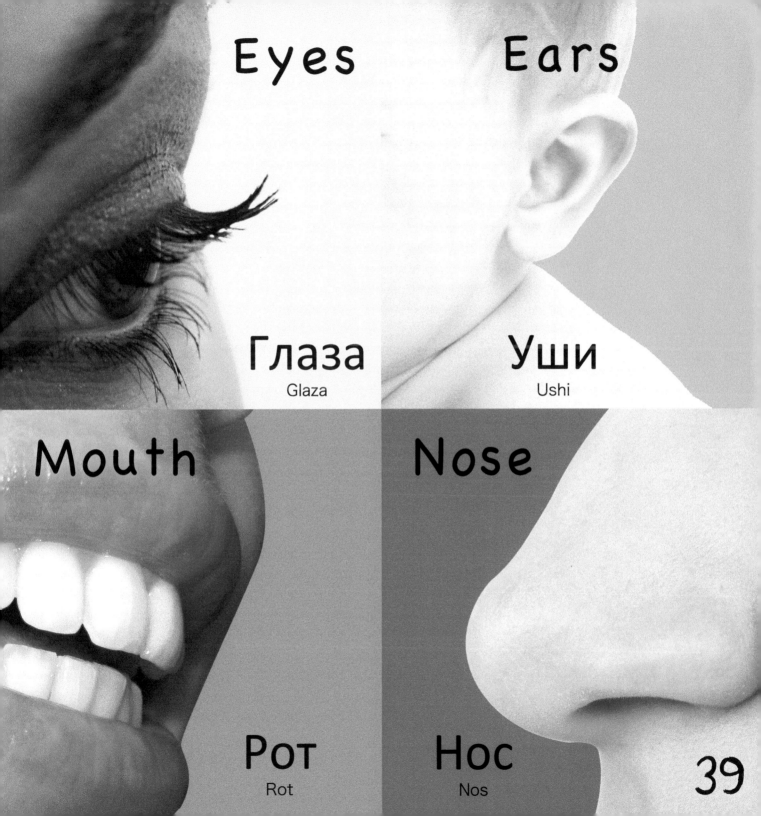

Eyes

Ears

Глаза
Glaza

Уши
Ushi

Mouth

Nose

Рот
Rot

Нос
Nos

39

Sippy cup

Чашка-непроливайка

Chashka nepralivayka

Bowl

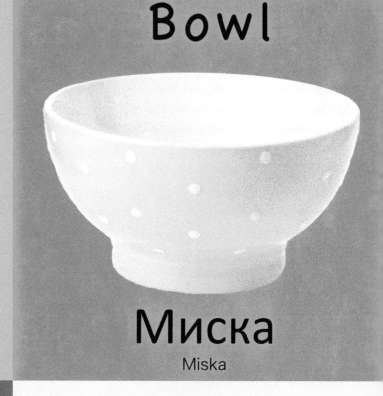

Миска

Miska

Pot

Кастрюля

Kastryulya

40

Cup

Кружка

Krushka

Plate

Тарелка

Tarelka

Fork

Вилка

Vilka

Knife

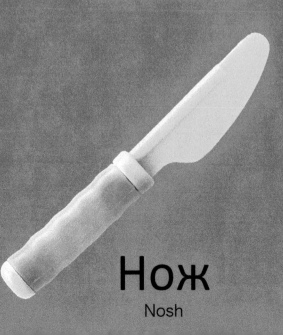

Нож

Nosh

Spoon

Ложка

Loshka

41

Hat

Шапка
Shapka

Shirt

Футболка
Fudbolka

Pants

Штаны
Shtany

Shorts

Шорты
Shorty

42

Gloves

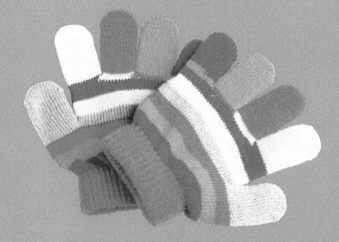

Перчатки

Pirchatki

Sunglasses

Солнцезащитные очки

Sontsezashcitnyye achki

Socks

Носки

Naski

Shoes

Обувь

Obuf'

43

Bath time
Время купания
Vremya kupaniya

Bath
Ванна
Vanna

Soap
Мыло
Mylo

Rubber duck

Резиновая утка
Rizinavaya utka

44

Brush

Чистить зубы

Chistit' zuby

Bed time
Время сна

Vremya sna

Book

Книга

Kniga

Potty

Пустячный

Pustyachnyy

Bed

Кровать

kravat'

45

THE Toddler's handbook

Match the following to the pictures below.
Can you find **7 pumpkins, a hooting owl,
a rainbow, a baseball, a lion, square blocks,
a sad boy, a helicopter, and shoes?**

Сопоставьте следующее с картинками ниже.
Можете ли вы найти 7 тыкв, сову,
радугу, бейсбол, льва, квадратные блоки,
грустного мальчика, вертолет и обувь?

ВЕРТОЛЁТ / helicopter
virtalYot

ТУФЛИ / shoes
tufli

СОВА / hooting owl
sava

БЕЙСБОЛ / baseball
beysbol

7 ТЫКВ / 7 pumpkins
7 tykv

ГРУСТНЫЙ МАЛЬЧИК / sad boy
grustnyy mal'chik

46 ЛЕВ / lion
lef

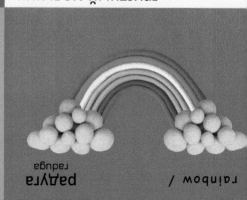

КВАДРАТНЫЕ БЛОКИ / square blocks
kvadratnyye bloki

РАДУГА / rainbow
raduga

Find more early concept books at www.engagebooks.com

About the Author

Dayna Martin is the mother of three young boys. When she finished writing *The Toddler's Handbook* her oldest son was 18 months old, and she had newborn twins. Following the successful launch of her first book, Dayna began work on *The Baby's Handbook*, *The Preschooler's Handbook*, and *The Kindergartener's Handbook*. The ideas in her books were inspired by her search to find better ways to teach her children. The concepts were vetted by numerous educators in different grade levels. Dayna is a stay-at-home mom, and is passionate about teaching her children in innovative ways. Her experiences have inspired her to create resources to help other families. With thousands of copies sold, her books have already become a staple learning source for many children around the world.

Translations

ASL (SIGN)	ITALIAN
ARABIC	JAPANESE
DUTCH	KOREAN
FILIPINO	MANDARIN
FRENCH	POLISH
GERMAN	PORTUGUESE
GREEK	RUSSIAN
HEBREW	SPANISH
HINDI	VIETNAMESE

Have comments or suggestions?
Contact us at: alexis@engagebooks.ca

 Show us how you enjoy your #handbook. Tweet a picture to @engagebooks for a chance to win free prizes.

CPSIA information can be obtained
at www.ICGtesting.com
Printed in the USA
BVHW020512230121
598528BV00007B/28